Hope for the Elephants

By Patricia J. Murphy

Penguin
Random
House

LONDON, NEW YORK, MUNICH,
MELBOURNE, AND DELHI

DK LONDON
Series Editor Deborah Lock
US Senior Editor Shannon Beatty
Project Art Editor Hoa Luc
Producer, Pre-production Francesca Wardell
Illustrator Hoa Luc

Reading Consultant
Linda Gambrell, Ph.D.

Subject Consultant
Matthew Lewis

DK DELHI
Editor Pomona Zaheer
Art Editor Yamini Panwar
DTP Designers Anita Yadav, Vijay Kandwal
Picture Researcher Aditya Katyal
Managing Editor Soma B. Chowdhury
Managing Art Editor Ahlawat Gunjan

First American Edition, 2015
Published in the United States by DK Publishing
345 Hudson Street, New York, New York 10014

14 15 16 17 10 9 8 7 6 5 4 3 2 1
001—273242—January/2015

Copyright © 2015 Dorling Kindersley Limited
All rights reserved. Without limiting the rights under copyright reserved above, no part of this p ublication may be
reproduced, stored in or introduced into a retrieval system, or transmitted, in any form, or by any means (electronic,
mechanical, photocopying, recording, or otherwise), without the prior written permission of the copyright owner.

Published in Great Britain by Dorling Kindersley Limited.

A catalog record for this book is availablefrom the Library of Congress.
ISBN: 978-1-4654-2842-4 (Paperback)
ISBN: 978-1-4654-2841-7 (Hardback)

DK books are available at special discounts when purchased in bulk for sales promotions,
premiums, fund-raising, or educational use. For details, contact:
DK Publishing Special Markets
345 Hudson Street, New York, New York 10014
SpecialSales@dk.com

Printed and bound in China by South China Printing Company.

The publisher would like to thank the following for their kind permission to reproduce their photographs:
(Key: a-above; b-below/bottom; c-center; f-far; l-left; r-right; t-top)
1 **Corbis**: Minden Pictures/Tui De Roy. 3 **Corbis**: Frans Lanting (br). 5 **Corbis**: Minden Pictures/Suzi Eszterhas (br); **Dorling
Kindersley**: Rough Guides (bc); **Dreamstime.com**: Prapass Wannapinij (camera with photographs). 6 **Dreamstime.com**:
Sutichak (bc/notebook). 7 **Corbis**: Image Source (t). 8–9 **Dreamstime.com**: Isaxar (bl, br). 10 **Getty Images**: Lonely Planet Images/
Diana Mayfield (b). 14–15 **Alamy Images**: Claudia Wiens (b); **Dreamstime.com**: Isaxar (bl, br). 18–19 **Dreamstime.com**:
Isaxar (bl, br).19 **Alamy Images**: age fotostock (bl); Images of Africa Photobank (br); **Corbis**: Laura Doss (cl); Westend61/Frank
Muckenheim (tl); Nature Picture Library/Jeff Vanuga (cra); **Getty Images**: Diane Seddon Photography (cr); Stone/Matthias
Clamer (tr); The Image Bank/Dkal Inc. (cla). 22 **Dorling Kindersley**: Rough Guides (b). 24 **Getty Images**: IWM via Getty Images (cr);
Lonely Planet Images/Paul Beinssen (br). 24–25 **Dreamstime.com**: Isaxar (bl, br). 25 **Alamy Images**: Danita Delimont (ca).
The Bridgeman Art Library: Elephants of the Raja of Travandrum, from 'Voyage in India', engraved by Louis Henri de Rudder
(1807–81), Soltykoff, A. (19th century) (after)/Private Collection/The Stapleton Collection/The Bridgeman Art Library (tl);
Getty Images: Lonely Planet Images/Grant Dixon (bl, cb). 26 **Getty Images**: British Library/Robana via Getty Images (c).
26–27 **Dreamstime.com**: Isaxar (bl, br). 27 **Alamy Images**: Heritage Image Partnership Ltd (crb); **Getty Images**: Stockbyte/Dinodia
Photos (tl). 29 **Katherine Connor**: (c). 30–31 **Dreamstime.com**: Isaxar (bl, br). 32–33 **Dreamstime.com**: Isaxar (bl, br). 38 **Alamy
Images**: RGB Ventures LLC dba SuperStock (b). 40 **Getty Images**: Photolibrary/Mark Carwardine (b). 42 **Corbis**: Theo Allofs (cr);
Getty Images: Photolibrary/Doug Cheeseman (cl). 42–43 **Dreamstime.com**: Isaxar (bl, br). 43 **Corbis**: Frans Lanting (bl); Ocean (cla);
Minden Pictures/Yva Momatiuk & John Eastcott (cra). 44 **Getty Images**: Ryan Goebel (b). 46 **Getty Images**: Barcroft Media via Getty
Images (b). 47 **Getty Images**: Barcroft Media via Getty Images (t). 48 **Getty Images**: Digital Vision/Anup Shah (br); Oxford
Scientific/Martyn Colbeck (cl). 48–49 **Dreamstime.com**: Vvoevale (Photo Frames Used Around All the Five Images); Isaxar (bl, br).
49 **Corbis**: Reuters/Laszlo Balogh (bl); Robert Harding World Imagery/James Hager (cr); **Getty Images**: The Image Bank/
Keren Su (tl). 51 **PunchStock**: Digital Vision/VisionsofAmerica/Joe Sohm (t). 52 **Getty Images**: Stockbyte/Tom Brakefield (b).
54–55 **Dreamstime.com**: Isaxar (bl, br). 56 **Corbis**: Frans Lanting (cl); Minden Pictures/ZSSD (cr, bc). 56–57 **Dreamstime.com**:
Isaxar (bl, br). 57 **Corbis**: Minden Pictures/ZSSD (tl, c); Theo Allofs (cra). 58–59 **Dreamstime.com**: Isaxar (bl, br).
60–61 **Dreamstime.com**: Isaxar (bl, br). 62–63 **Dreamstime.com**: Isaxar (bl, br).
Jacket images: Front: Corbis: Minden Pictures/Yva Momatiuk & John Eastcott; **Spine: Getty Images**: Barcroft Media via Getty Images

All other images © Dorling Kindersley
For further information see: www.dkimages.com

Discover more at
www.dk.com

Contents

My name is David. I am what you might call an elephant expert. I collect facts about elephants like my friends collect baseball cards. It all began when my Grandma Jo gave me a toy elephant, which I named Babar.

My grandma works at a museum
that teaches about animals.
She's creating an exhibit on
the future of elephants.
She's worried about them.
I am, too.

Grandma is traveling to Asia and Africa to study the problems elephants are facing. She promised we'd see elephants in the wild someday. She invited me along as her helper. Of course I said, "Yes!"

We updated our passports, booked our flights, and started packing.

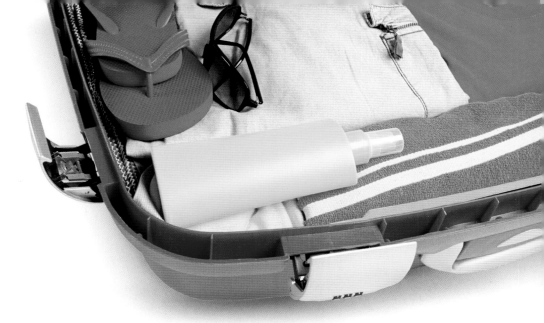

Grandma said to me, "You'll need to take clothes that you don't mind getting muddy, torn, or covered with elephant goo."
So I packed T-shirts, shorts, pants, sneakers, flip-flops, a notebook, a camera, and Babar.

I'll be writing about my trip in the notebook and including photographs and pictures.

First Stop: Asia

This map shows where populations of wild Asian elephants can be found. They used to live in many more places and in much larger numbers.

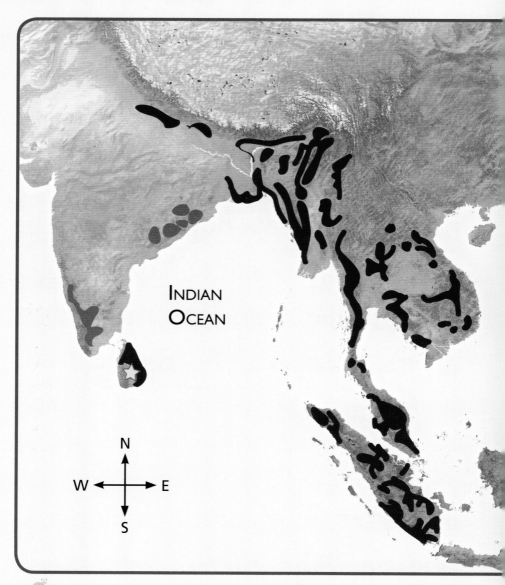

INDIAN OCEAN

N
W ← → E
S

This elephant sanctuary in Sri Lanka is one of many sanctuaries in Asia. Here tame elephants are cared for in a large enclosed natural habitat where they can live safely.

PACIFIC OCEAN

● Half of the total world population of wild Asian elephants (about 18,000) live in India, and half of these live in southwest India. These elephants roam freely.

● Other main populations of wild elephants (between 1,000 and 5,000) live in forests across Southeast Asia. Some of these areas have become national parks or reserves where the elephants can be protected.

Settling In
Date: February 21st

We flew for nearly 17 hours and then rode on a rickety bus for six more hours to the elephant sanctuary in Sri Lanka.

Stella, the owner, greeted us
at the wide front gates and
gave us a tour of the place.
She said that she first came to
Sri Lanka to volunteer ten years
ago, and then decided to stay.
That's what I would like to do.
Grandma told me not to get
any ideas!

Date: February 22nd

At the welcome breakfast on our first morning, we learned the three sanctuary rules:

1. EVERYTHING is about the elephants. We are here to serve them. They are here to be happy!

2. NO shouting, crowding, or approaching the elephants. They will come to you!

3. LISTEN to the mahouts (the elephant handlers) at all times!

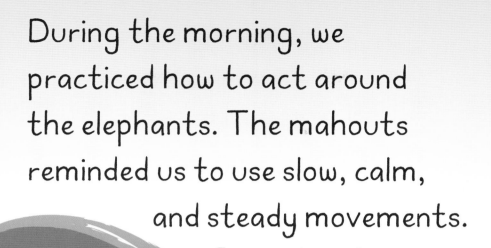

During the morning, we practiced how to act around the elephants. The mahouts reminded us to use slow, calm, and steady movements. I practiced over and over again. Elephants, here I come!

Join Us as a Volunteer

Help us care for more than
30 elephants for a week or longer!

Here are a few highlights of volunteering:

 watch elephants being elephants!
Sit, watch, and enjoy these majestic
and amazing creatures.

 work with our staff to keep our
elephants' habitat in the best condition,
by fixing fences, cleaning
the enclosure, and making repairs.

 hand-feed the elephants their favorite
food, including bananas. Watch out!
They will keep coming back for more.

Here are some of the things you can do:

 bathe and clean the elephants in a river. You'll get a bath doing this, too!

 scoop up elephant dung. It's everywhere! Each elephant drops approximately 210 lb (95 kg) every day, so watch your step!

 collect elephant food. Visit local farms to cut corn and slash grass.

 help out in the elephant kitchen. Unload food from trucks, wash pumpkins, and stack bananas.

Make a difference to the lives of our elephants.

Date: February 23rd

We took turns with the other volunteers to clean the enclosures where the elephants slept, gather their food, round them up, and bathe them.

While planting some young trees, I saw my first sanctuary elephant. I kept repeating, "slow, calm, and steady."
It came close, reached out its trunk, and oozed something all over me. (It was elephant snot!) I didn't mind.

I stared into its soft brown eyes. I can't imagine anyone wanting to hurt these wonderful creatures!

How are Elephants and Humans Alike?

Memory
We both can have very long memories.

Emotion
We both show a range of emotions, including smiling and crying.

Communication
We both use gestures, such as those for greeting and comforting.

Intelligence
We both behave and act cleverly, and learn from our experiences.

Life span
We both have long lives. Elephants can live to around 70 years old.

Here are a few of the similarities between elephants and humans.

Humans	Elephants

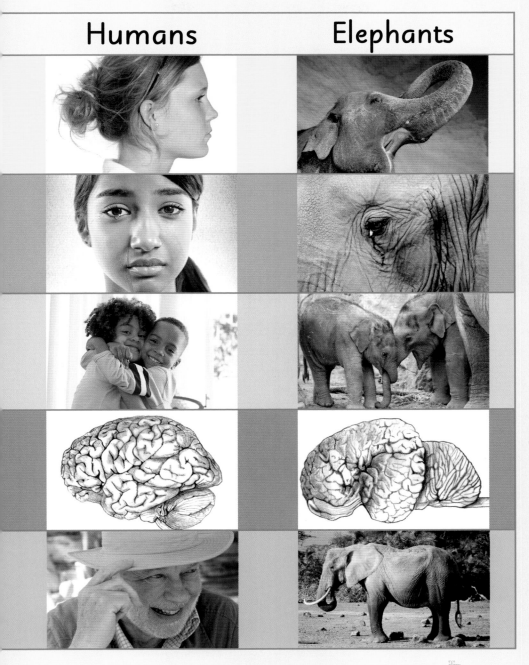

Getting to Know Elephants

Date: February 24th

Each elephant we meet has a different life story. Donnie worked long hours pulling up trees for the logging industry. Lizzie carried tourists on steep treks through mountains, and Ollie performed in shows. When their bodies could no longer work, they joined their mahouts on the streets begging for money.

Thanks to Stella's sanctuary, these elephants can now live in a natural habitat, enjoying freedom and friendship and having fun!

Date: February 25th

At daybreak, we joined Stella while she met with the local villagers to ask for their help with the elephants. Afterward, under the hot sun, we walked the elephants to the river.

The mahouts made sure they stayed together and didn't stray outside the grounds of the sanctuary.

Stella hopes to secure more land for the elephants. She hopes they will return to the wild someday. But in the wild, they'd face the same dangers that wild Asian elephants do. They'd have smaller areas in which to roam, have to compete for food, and may be captured for work or killed by poachers.

History of Elephants

For 4,000 years, Asian elephants have been an important part of life for people in Asia. People have captured, reared, and trained them for specific purposes. These wild animals lost their freedom.

On the battlefield

Elephants have been used by armies for transportation and to scare away the enemy.

Religious ceremony

Elephants continue to be decorated in cloth, bells, and necklaces for festival processions. They carry people and the relics.

Travel and exploration

In the 19th century, jungle explorers rode elephants and used them to carry their equipment.

Forest work

Even today elephants are used for logging work because of their strength.

Entertainment

Elephants have been and continue to be trained as circus performers. Some countries have now banned this.

Tourism

Even today elephant rides are popular with tourists, especially for trips into the jungle on safaris to look for tigers.

Elephants as Gods

The size and power of elephants have inspired people to respect and worship these creatures as gods.

Airavata

As the king of the Hindu gods, Lord Indra is shown flying Airavata, a magnificent white elephant.

Ganesha

In Hindu tradition, this very popular elephant-headed god helps people achieve success by taking away their problems.

African elephant fables

In West African countries, such as Ghana and Cameroon, the elephant in fables represents a wise chief settling arguments in the forest. This headdress is worn for tribal ceremonies.

Date: February 26th

On our last day in Asia, Grandma Jo and I spent the whole time with the elephants—walking, eating, and even swimming with them! Did you know elephants use their trunks as snorkels?

On our way back to the enclosure, we passed a memorial covered with fresh flowers.

Stella explained that this memorial honors elephants they could not—and cannot—save. Grandma Jo and I took a minute to remember all the people trying to save the elephants.

Elephant Trunk Tricks

An elephant's trunk is its nose. Besides smelling and breathing, here are some other things an elephant can do with its trunk.

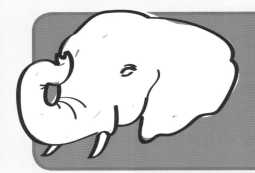

Touch its head to show who is in charge or show care for its young.

Wrestle with another bull (male) elephant to show its strength and gain a mate.

Stretch and reach for water to wash and spray itself.

Delicately remove grit, sand, or soil out of its eyes.

Grip things for eating. An African elephant has a two-finger grip.

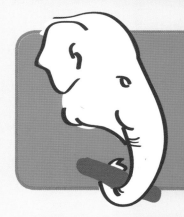

Curl things for carrying. An Asian elephant only has a one-finger grip.

Rest on its ivory tusks when it is tired.

Next Stop: Africa

Once African elephants were found across most of Africa. There may have been as many as 3–5 million of them. Today the number of elephants has fallen due to poachers hunting for trophies and tusks, smaller areas for roaming, and elephant groups being split up.

 This wildlife reserve in Kenya is one of many protected areas for African elephants in the wild.

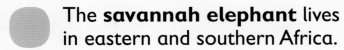 The **forest elephant** is found in the tropical rain forest zone of western and central Africa.

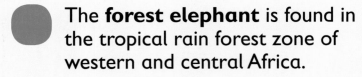 The **savannah elephant** lives in eastern and southern Africa.

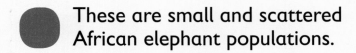 These are small and scattered African elephant populations.

Good news! The elephant populations in southern Africa are large and getting larger. About 300,000 elephants now roam across the area.

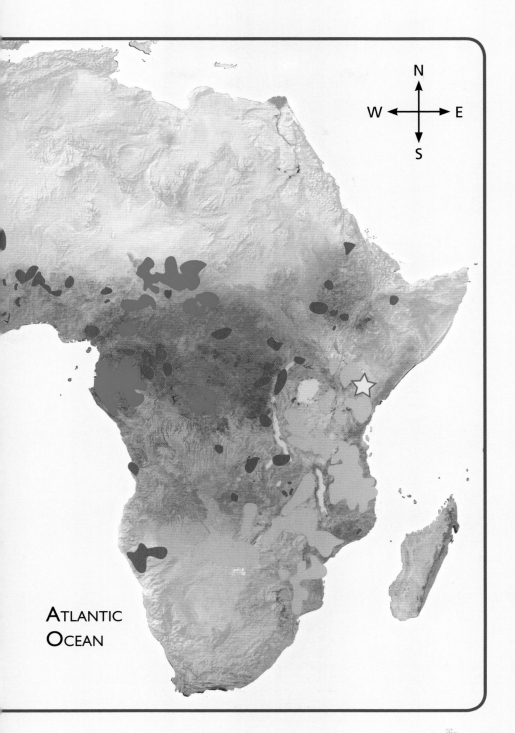

N
W ← → E
S

ATLANTIC
OCEAN

Learning About Elephants

Date: February 27th

After our nine-hour flight to Kenya and a short, bumpy drive, we arrived at the nature reserve.

The first people we met were members of the reserve's anti-poaching patrol. We learned that thousands of African elephants are being poached for their ivory tusks every year! The reserve is working all day and night to change this. Grandma and I tried to fight back tears when we heard the stories, but we couldn't.

Date: February 27th

We learned that African elephants are also losing their habitats and their lives, competing with humans for land and food. Some of the reserve staff are teaching the local villagers ways to prevent elephants from raiding their crops or trampling their farmland.

Some solutions include building fences, growing chili peppers, and hanging beehives on trees. Elephants will stay away from all three of these things.

Date: February 28th

Today we joined the busy researchers tracking the reserve's elephants to find out about their movements and behaviors and how they could be protected.

Elephant being tagged with an electronic device.

Some researchers tag the elephants with special collars. This helps them to record where the elephants roam. Others study their dung to find out what the elephants eat! They also record their sounds. Elephants make loud trumpeting and low rumbling sounds, which are lower than we can hear. They make these noises to stay connected with their family nearby and far away.

Date: February 28th

Suddenly, word came that an elephant was trapped in a snare! The de-snaring team and mobile veterinary unit raced to save it. First they calmed the elephant with a sleeping drug.

Then they removed the wire snare before cleaning and stitching the elephant's wounds. Soon the elephant was as good as new and could return to the wild— but there's still the danger of this happening again. Snares are everywhere!

A Day in the Life of a Savannah Elephant

From dawn to dusk, elephants roam the African savannah, searching for and eating large amounts of food.

6:00 AM

Feeding: an elephant digs in the soil for salt. Salt is an important part of its diet.

11:00 AM

Showering: a dust shower helps to keep the insects away.

1:00 PM

Bathing: elephants cool down from the midday heat in a mudbath.

6:00 PM

More feeding: a branch, or even a whole tree, makes a tasty evening meal.

10:00 PM

Drinking: elephants take an evening stroll to the waterhole for another drink of water.

Protecting the Elephants

Date: March 1st

Today was "field trip day" at the reserve's orphan nursery! We joined children from nearby schools to watch orphaned

elephants take mudbaths, and to learn how we can all be elephant protectors.

Soon after, we met a girl named Daphne. Her father works as one of the nursery's elephant keepers. The keepers act as the orphans' family members. Most of the orphans lost their mothers to poachers in the African savannah.

Date: March 1st

We visited the places where the orphans and keepers sleep, eat, and play. The orphans are never left alone!

An orphan needs a lot of love and care...

... and special milk to stay alive.

One day, they'll grow up to join the reserve's wild elephants. Daphne and I fed the orphan, Edwin, a bottle. Grandma and I sang him to sleep with an Irish lullaby. It was the same one Grandma used to sing to me!

Big Babies Gallery

From the moment elephants are born, they are a big part of the family. They are cared for by their mothers, aunts, and other members of the herd. Their survival depends on this.

A big welcome

Welcome to the world! I'll be up on my feet soon.

Healthy drinks

I get tired and thirsty following my mom around all day. Luckily, she's always close by for a drink.

Endless play time

A piggyback ride at mudbath time is so much fun! There's a good view from here. Whoops, I'm slipping!

Plenty of snuggles

The best place to snuggle and rest is curled up right next to my mom!

Family reunions

Spending time with my whole herd is the best time of all. One day, I'll be as big as my mom!

Date: March 2nd

On our final day of the trip, we traveled through the reserve one last time with a tour guide. He was from the local village. Ecotourism is one way that villagers can make money and save the pachyderms [PA-ki-derms]. (That's a BIG word for elephants!)

Elephant-friendly tours allow visitors to see elephants in their natural habitats. They can enjoy elephants just being elephants. There are no rides or tricks.

Date: March 2nd

At sunset, we joined the reserve staff for a good-bye dinner of chili and honey biscuits. We were reminded that they were made with the villagers' chili peppers and honey from their bees!

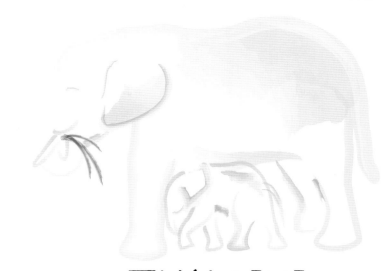

TUMAINI

Before leaving, Daphne handed me a picture she drew with the word "TUMAINI," which means hope. She told us that it's now our job to spread the word—and be the hope for the elephants! We all agreed that's what the elephants will need.

Why Do Elephants Matter?

Elephants are the largest land animals. Plants and other animals depend upon them in many ways.

Plant dispersal and growth

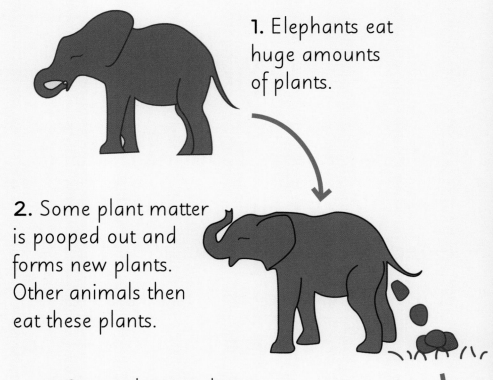

1. Elephants eat huge amounts of plants.

2. Some plant matter is pooped out and forms new plants. Other animals then eat these plants.

3. Some plant seeds need to go through the digestive system of elephants to be able to start growing.

Fresh water

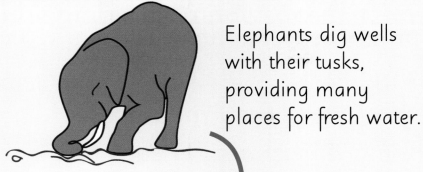

Elephants dig wells with their tusks, providing many places for fresh water.

Other animals then use these wells.

Forest growth

Elephants make trails across a large area. As they move around, they knock down large plants.

Smaller plants are then able to grow in the sunlight.

Naming Elephants

Some researchers can identify as many as 500 elephants on one reserve. They may use the shapes and characteristics of the elephants' ears.

Van Gogh

Monet

Renoir

Newton

Einstein

Beethoven

Mozart

Choosing names

Researchers often use memorable names like famous musicians, scientists, or artists to remember and identify the elephants.

Spread the Hope

You can be the hope for elephants, too.

 Don't buy anything made of ivory or that looks like ivory, and tell your family and friends not to buy them either.

 Don't buy products that harm elephants' natural habitats. Instead, choose paper and wood products with the Forest Stewardship Council (FSC) sign.

 Don't visit places where elephants are forced to perform tricks or work hard.

 Do visit national parks, or reserves and sanctuaries, that promote elephant-friendly tourism and jobs for villagers.

 Do sponsor an orphaned elephant at a sanctuary or raise money for the World Wildlife Fund or other organizations that help to save and protect elephants.

Elephants Quiz

1. In which country does half of the Asian elephant population live?

2. What is an elephant handler called?

3. What is the name of the Hindu elephant-headed god?

4. Name two things an elephant can do with its trunk.

5. How do researchers track the movements of elephants in the reserve?

Answers on page 61.

Glossary

ecotourism
trips to watch wildlife without harming their habitats

exhibit
display of objects

mahout
someone who trains and handles elephants

mobile veterinary unit
vets traveling around in a vehicle containing medical equipment for helping animals

orphan
child whose parents have died

pachyderm
large hoofed mammal with thick skin

poaching
killing and stealing animals without permission

reserve
protected area set aside for animals

sanctuary
place of safety

savannah
large area of flat grassland in hot countries with a few trees

snare
trap for capturing animals

volunteer
someone who does a job without getting paid

Index

Answers to the Elephants Quiz:
1. India; **2**. Mahout; **3**. Ganesha;
4. Answers found on pages 30–31;
5. Tag with an electronic device on a collar.

Guide for Parents

DK Readers is a four-level interactive reading adventure series for children, developing the habit of reading widely for both pleasure and information. These books have an exciting main narrative interspersed with a range of reading genres to suit your child's reading ability, as required by the Common Core State Standards. Each book is designed to develop your child's reading skills, fluency, grammar awareness, and comprehension in order to build confidence and engagement when reading.

Ready for a *Reading Alone* book

YOUR CHILD SHOULD

- be able to read most words without needing to stop and break them down into sound parts.
- read smoothly, in phrases and with expression. By this level, your child will be mostly reading silently.
- self-correct when some word or sentence doesn't sound right.

A VALUABLE AND SHARED READING EXPERIENCE

For some children, text reading, particularly non-fiction, requires much effort, but adult participation can make this both fun and easier. So here are a few tips on how to use this book with your child.

TIP 1 Check out the contents together before your child begins:

- invite your child to check the blurb, contents page, and layout of the book and comment on it.
- ask your child to make predictions about the story.
- talk about the information your child might want to find out.

TIP 2 Encourage fluent and flexible reading:

- support your child to read in fluent, expressive phrases, making full use of punctuation and thinking about the meaning.

- encourage your child to slow down and check information where appropriate.

TIP 3 Indicators that your child is reading for meaning:

- your child will be responding to the text if he/she is self-correcting and varying his/her voice.
- your child will want to talk about what he/she is reading or is eager to turn the page to find out what will happen next.

TIP 4 Share and discuss:

- encourage your child to recall specific details after each chapter.
- provide opportunities for your child to pick out interesting words and discuss what they mean.
- discuss how the author captures the reader's interest, or how effective the non-fiction layouts are.
- ask questions about the text. These help to develop comprehension skills and awareness of the language used.

A FEW ADDITIONAL TIPS

- Read to your child regularly to demonstrate fluency, phrasing, and expression; to find out or check information; and for sharing enjoyment.
- Encourage your child to reread favorite texts to increase reading confidence and fluency.
- Check that your child is reading a range of different types of material, such as poems, jokes, and following instructions.

Series consultant, **Dr. Linda Gambrell**, Distinguished Professor of Education at Clemson University, has served as President of the National Reading Conference, the College Reading Association, and the International Reading Association. She is also reading consultant for the **DK Adventures**.

Have you read these other great books from DK?

Meet the sharks
who live on the
reef or come
passing through.

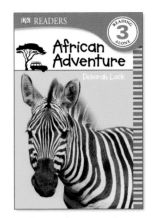

Experience the
thrill of seeing
wild animals on
an African safari.

Through Zoe's
blog, discover the
mysteries of the
Amazon.

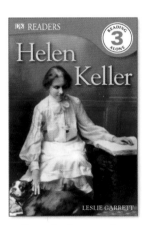

Read about the
remarkable story
of the deaf-blind
girl who achieved
great things.

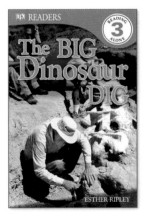

Josh and his team
dig up dinosaur
bones in a race
against time.

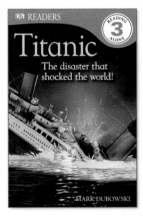

This is the
incredible true
story of the
"unsinkable" ship
that sank.